ROCKS

BY SALLY M. WALKER

LERNER PUBLICATIONS COMPANY • MINNEAPOLIS

Lerner Publications Company
A division of Lerner Publishing Group
241 First Avenue North
Minneapolis, MN 55401 U.S.A

Website address: www.lernerbooks.com

Library of Congress Cataloging-in-Publication Data

Walker, Sally M.
    Rocks / by Sally M. Walker.
        p.   cm. — (Early bird Earth science)
    Includes index.
    Summary: Describes the structure and function of the human circulatory system
    ISBN-13: 978-0-8225-5947-4 (lib. bdg. : alk. paper)
    ISBN-10: 0-8225-5947-1 (lib. bdg. : alk. paper)
    1. Rocks—Juvenile literature. I. Title. II. Series.
QE432.2.W345 2007
552—dc22   2005032220

Manufactured in the United States of America
1 2 3 4 5 6 – JR – 12 11 10 09 08 07

CONTENTS

BE A WORD DETECTIVE

Can you find these words as you read about rocks? Be a
detective and try to figure out what they mean. You can
turn to the glossary on page 46 for help.

cementing	lava	rock cycle
crust	magma	sedimentary
crystals	metamorphic	rocks
cycle	rocks	sediments
fossils	minerals	weathering
igneous rocks	plates	

CHAPTER 1
WHAT IS A ROCK?

Rocks are everywhere you look. Mountains made of rock point at the sky. And rocks rattle and roll across the ground. A rock can be bigger than your house. Or it can be tiny, like a grain of sand on a beach.

Sheets of rock lie just beneath Earth's soil and water. These sheets of rock are called Earth's crust. The crust is Earth's outer layer. Most of the inside of Earth is made of rock too.

Most of the rocks we see are pieces that have broken off of Earth's crust.

Talc is very soft. Any other mineral can scratch it.

Rocks are made of minerals (MIHN-ur-uhlz). A mineral is a solid substance that is not alive. Minerals form inside Earth. More than 3,500 different kinds of minerals are found on Earth.

Some minerals are soft. Talc is a soft mineral. You could scratch it with your fingernail. Some baby powder is made of ground-up talc.

Other minerals are hard. Quartz is a hard mineral. You would have to hit quartz with a hammer to break it. Diamond is the hardest mineral of all. A hard mineral can scratch any softer mineral. So diamond can scratch any other mineral.

Most quartz is clear, like glass. This piece of clear quartz has thin lines running through it.

Purple quartz is called amethyst (AM-uh-thist).

Minerals can be many different colors. A rock gets its color from the minerals it's made of. Some minerals come in more than one color. Quartz is usually clear. But it may be pink, gray, or purple.

The mineral feldspar can be pink. The mineral mica (MY-kuh) can be gray or black. When the minerals feldspar, mica, and quartz are mixed together, they become a kind of rock called granite (GRAN-it). Some granite is pink. Pink granite has a lot of feldspar in it. And some granite is gray. Gray granite has a lot of mica in it.

Granite rock can be many different colors.

Pumice (PUH-muhs) rock is full of holes. Pumice is made from melted rock. What do we call melted rock that is inside Earth?

CHAPTER 2
IGNEOUS ROCKS

There are three groups of rocks on Earth. All rocks belong to one of these groups.

Igneous (IHG-nee-uhs) rocks are one group. Igneous rocks are made deep inside Earth, where it is very hot. It is so hot that rocks melt!

Melted rock that is inside Earth is called magma (MAG-muh). Magma isn't solid. Instead, it is soft, like toothpaste or thick syrup. Magma doesn't stay in one place. It moves around inside Earth. It pushes up toward Earth's surface. It squeezes into cracks in hard rock.

Melted rock is thick and gooey.

When melted rock cools, it becomes hard.

Liquid water changes into solid ice when it is cooled. When magma is cooled, it becomes solid rock. Earth's crust is much cooler than magma. So hot magma cools when it moves into the crust. The magma changes into solid rock. The cooled magma has become igneous rock.

Sometimes magma flows out of holes in Earth's crust. It spills out onto Earth's surface. Then the melted rock is called lava (LAH-vuh). The holes lava flows out of are called volcanoes. Very hot lava is bright orange and yellow. As it flows across the ground, it looks like a fiery river. Lava's color becomes darker and darker as it cools. When lava gets cool enough, it becomes solid. It turns into igneous rock.

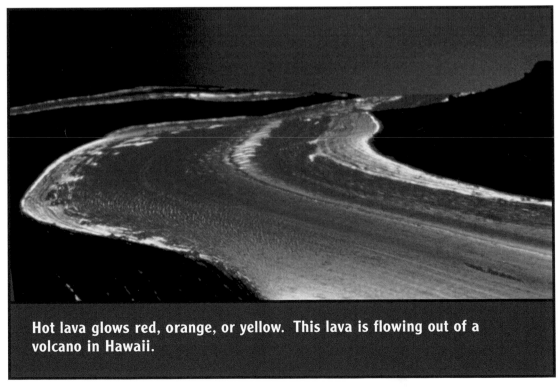

Hot lava glows red, orange, or yellow. This lava is flowing out of a volcano in Hawaii.

Round lumps of hardened lava are called pillow lava because they look sort of like pillows.

Lava oozes from cracks along the ocean floor too. Cold seawater quickly cools the lava. Sometimes the lava hardens into round, pillow-shaped rocks.

As melted rock cools, the minerals it is made of may form crystals (KRIHS-tuhlz). Crystals are solid shapes. They have many flat surfaces. Each flat surface is called a face. Some igneous rocks have many flat, shiny bits in them. The shiny bits are crystal faces.

These crystals have many long, narrow faces.

It takes time for a crystal to form. When a crystal begins to form, it is very tiny. Slowly, the crystal grows bigger.

It took a while for these large crystals to grow.

This igneous rock is called pegmatite. It cooled slowly, so it has large crystals.

The crystals in an igneous rock tell us about the melted rock it was made from. Sometimes melted rock cools slowly. Other times, melted rock cools quickly. Crystals can help you figure out whether a rock cooled slowly or quickly.

Some igneous rocks have large crystals. What does that tell you? It tells you that these rocks cooled slowly. The crystals had a lot of time to grow.

Other igneous rocks have tiny crystals. Can you guess what that means? It means that these rocks cooled more quickly. The crystals did not have time to grow big.

The rhyolite (RYE-oh-lite) rock on the left has smaller crystals than the granite on the right. So the rhyolite cooled more quickly than the granite.

Obsidian rock is smooth, like glass. Most obsidian is black.

Some igneous rocks have no crystals at all. They cooled so quickly that crystals didn't have time to start growing.

One kind of igneous rock is called obsidian (ahb-SIH-dee-uhn). It is as smooth as glass. Obsidian has no crystals at all. Do you think obsidian forms when lava cools slowly or when it cools quickly?

Some rock is made of small pieces of mud, sand, or stones. What are these pieces called?

CHAPTER 3

SEDIMENTARY ROCKS

The second group of rocks are called
sedimentary (SEH-duh-MEHN-tuh-ree) rocks.
Sedimentary rocks form on Earth's surface or just

beneath it. They are made of small pieces called sediments (SEH-duh-muhnts). Some sediments are bits of mud, sand, or small stones. Other sediments are shells or pieces of bone. When sediments harden together, they become sedimentary rock.

Wind and rain can break tiny pieces off of large rocks. The pieces are sediments. You can see piles of sediments at the bottom of this rocky cliff.

When the water in a river slows down, it can no longer carry sediments with it. The sediments fall to the bottom. Sometimes the sediments form big piles.

Sediments are always being moved to new places. Waves bounce sediments along the bottom of rivers and oceans. Wind sweeps them across the land. Mountains of ice slide sediments from one place to another.

Sediments pile up to form a layer. A layer of sediments can be on the land. Or it can be underwater.

A sand dune is a pile of sediments that have been blown by the wind.

New layers of sediments form on top of older ones. Sometimes the layers of sediments are different colors. If you could cut through the layers, they would look like stripes.

Sediment layers can be thousands of feet thick. Deep layers of sediments are heavy. The top layers press down on the bottom layers. The lower sediments are squeezed very tightly together. They become sedimentary rock.

The stripes in this rock are layers of sediments.

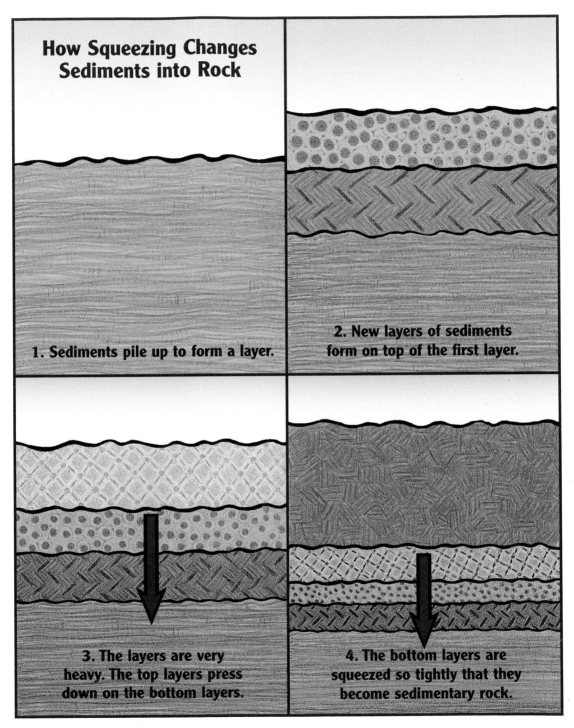

How Squeezing Changes Sediments into Rock

1. Sediments pile up to form a layer.

2. New layers of sediments form on top of the first layer.

3. The layers are very heavy. The top layers press down on the bottom layers.

4. The bottom layers are squeezed so tightly that they become sedimentary rock.

27

This rock is called breccia (BREH-chuh). It is made of small bits of rock that have been glued together.

Sometimes loose sediments are glued together to make rock. This is called cementing (sih-MEHN-tihng). Cementing starts when water seeps into the spaces between the sediments. Dissolved minerals are in the water. The dissolved minerals become hard. They glue the sediments together. The cemented sediments become sedimentary rock.

Sand grains can be cemented together to form a sedimentary rock called sandstone. Conglomerate (kuhn-GLAH-muh-ruht) is another kind of sedimentary rock. It has a mixture of different sizes of sediments. Large pebbles, small pebbles, and sand grains are cemented together.

Conglomerate rock is made of many different sizes of sediments.

Some of the shells in this piece of limestone have been broken into small pieces.

Limestone is a sedimentary rock made from shells. The shells are from animals such as clams and snails. After the animals die, their shells become sediments on the ocean bottom. Over time, they are cemented together. They become limestone.

Sedimentary rocks hold clues that tell where the rocks formed. Shale is a sedimentary rock made from mud. And mud is found near water. So a piece of shale may have started out as mud on a riverbank or on the bottom of a lake.

Shale often breaks into big, flat pieces.

This fossil is the bones of a dinosaur that lived millions of years ago.

Sedimentary rock sometimes has fossils in it. Fossils are bones or other traces of animals and plants that lived long ago. Fossils of dinosaur footprints are often found in shale. Dinosaurs' feet made footprints in soft mud, just like your feet would. The mud dried and became hard.

The shape of the footprints was saved in the hardened mud. Over time, the sediments in the mud were cemented together. The mud turned to shale. The dinosaurs' footprints can still be seen in the rock.

Fossil dinosaur tracks show the shape of the dinosaur's feet and how it walked.

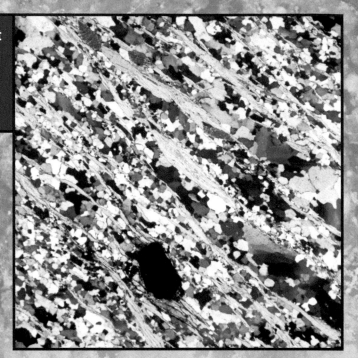

This rock is called schist (SHIST). Schist forms when another kind of rock changes. What can make a rock change?

CHAPTER 4
METAMORPHIC ROCKS

The third group of rocks are called metamorphic (MEH-tuh-MOR-fik) rocks. Metamorphic rocks are made out of other kinds of rock.

Rocks can change. A rock changes if it gets very hot, but not hot enough to melt. And a rock changes if it is squeezed very, very hard.

Heating and squeezing change the minerals inside the rock. The rock becomes a metamorphic rock.

Rocks that are near magma can get very hot. They do not get hot enough to melt. But the heat may change the minerals in the rocks. If the minerals change, the rocks become metamorphic rocks.

This rock was squeezed so hard that its layers bent!

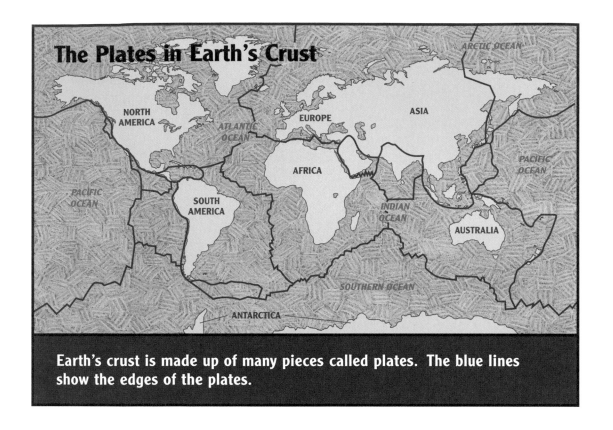

The Plates in Earth's Crust

Earth's crust is made up of many pieces called plates. The blue lines show the edges of the plates.

Rocks are pushed and squeezed inside Earth. Earth's crust is divided into large pieces called plates. The plates slowly move on Earth's surface. Sometimes the plates push against one another. This movement squeezes rocks tightly. Rocks that are under very deep layers of rock get squeezed too. The squeezing can change the rocks into metamorphic rock.

Limestone is a sedimentary rock. Limestone can be many colors, such as white, tan, and gray. Limestone often contains fossils of shells. When limestone gets very hot, it changes into a metamorphic rock called marble. When limestone changes into marble, the fossils in it disappear. Marble can be many different colors, such as pink, white, and black. It often has swirling lines in it.

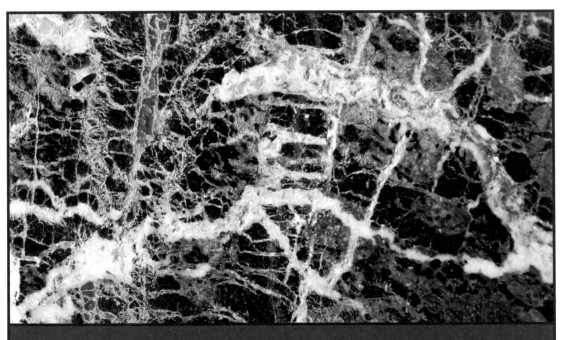

Marble is often used to make buildings and statues.

Gneiss (NICE) rock has many light and dark layers.

Granite is an igneous rock. It is made of bits of light-colored and dark-colored minerals. The bits are all jumbled up. When granite is squeezed hard, the minerals move. They separate into light and dark layers. The granite changes into a metamorphic rock called gneiss.

Shale is a sedimentary rock. Shale is usually gray or black. But it may be red, green, or brown. When shale is squeezed, its minerals line up in flat layers. The shale changes into a metamorphic rock called slate. Slate easily breaks apart into thin, flat pieces. Slate is usually a darker color than shale.

Slate breaks into thin, hard sheets. The sheets can be used to cover the roofs of buildings.

Each day, the sun rises in the morning and sets in the evening. What do we call things that happen over and over?

CHAPTER 5
THE ROCK CYCLE

The three groups of rocks are part of a cycle (SYE-kuhl). A cycle is a pattern that happens again and again. A day has a cycle. In this cycle, daytime changes into nighttime, then back to daytime. Rocks have a cycle too. The rock cycle changes old rocks into new ones.

Water, wind, and ice change rocks. These forces scrape and scratch rocks. And they crack rocks apart. These changes are called weathering (WEH-thur-ihng). Over millions of years, weathering can turn a mountain made of old igneous rock into sediments. The sediments can become new sedimentary rock.

Weathering made a huge hole in this rock. Now the rock looks sort of like a bridge.

Long ago, these layers of rock were flat. Then Earth's crust moved. The layers of rock were pushed so hard that they became tilted.

Heat changes rocks too. Earth's rocky crust is always moving. Most of the movements are too slow and small for us to see. But slowly, rocks are pulled and pushed into new places. Old sedimentary and metamorphic rocks can be pushed down inside Earth. When the old rocks get hot enough, they melt. They become magma. If the magma cools and hardens, it becomes new igneous rock.

Find a rock near your house or school. Look at it closely. Can you see crystals? Does the rock have pebbles in it? Try to figure out if it is an igneous rock, a sedimentary rock, or a metamorphic rock.

Rocks are everywhere. Look at the streets, buildings, and sidewalks around you. The many different rocks you see may surprise you!

This wall is made out of rocks.

ON SHARING A BOOK

When you share a book with a child, you show that reading is important. To get the most out of the experience, read in a comfortable, quiet place. Turn off the television and limit other distractions, such as telephone calls.

Be prepared to start slowly. Take turns reading parts of this book. Stop occasionally and discuss what you're reading. Talk about the photographs. If the child begins to lose interest, stop reading. When you pick up the book again, revisit the parts you have already read.

BE A VOCABULARY DETECTIVE

The word list on page 5 contains words that are important in understanding the topic of this book. Be word detectives and search for the words as you read the book together. Talk about what the words mean and how they are used in the sentence. Do any of these words have more than one meaning? You will find the words defined in a glossary on page 46.

WHAT ABOUT QUESTIONS?

Use questions to make sure the child understands the information in this book. Here are some suggestions:

> What did this paragraph tell us? What does this picture show? What are rocks made of? What is the difference between magma and lava? How do sediments change into sedimentary rock? What forces change rocks into metamorphic rocks? What is your favorite part of the book? Why?

If the child has questions, don't hesitate to respond with questions of your own, such as What do *you* think? Why? What is it that you don't know? If the child can't remember certain facts, turn to the index.

INTRODUCING THE INDEX

The index helps readers find information without searching through the whole book. Turn to the index on page 48. Choose an entry such as *igneous rock* and ask the child to use the index to find out what kind of rock is as smooth as glass. Repeat with as many entries as you like. Ask the child to point out the differences between an index and a glossary. (The index helps readers find information, while the glossary tells readers what words mean.)

LEARN MORE ABOUT
ROCKS

BOOKS

Anderson, Peter. *A Grand Canyon Journey: Tracing Time in Stone.* New York: Franklin Watts, 1997.

Hooper, Meredith. *The Pebble in My Pocket: A History of our Earth.* New York: Viking, 1996.

Spickert, Diane Nelson. *Earthsteps: A Rock's Journey through Time.* Golden, CO: Fulcrum Kids, 2000.

Stamper, Judith Bauer. *Rocky Road Trip.* New York: Scholastic Inc., 2003.

WEBSITES

If Rocks Could Talk!
http://ology.amnh.org/earth/ifrockscouldtalk/index.html
Every rock has a story to tell about Earth's history. This website has the stories of six different rocks, plus photos of igneous, sedimentary, and metamorphic rocks.

Mineral Matters
http://www.sdnhm.org/kids/minerals/
This website has information about minerals, instructions for growing your own crystals, puzzles, and more.

Neighborhood Rocks
http://www.saltthesandbox.org/rocks/index.htm
Learn all about rock collecting! This website includes descriptions of some kinds of rocks you might find in your neighborhood.

Rocks for Kids
http://www.rocksforkids.com/
This Web page has lots of information about rocks, including how to identify different kinds of rocks.

GLOSSARY

cementing (sih-MEHN-tihng): gluing together

crust: Earth's outer layer

crystals (KRIHS-tuhlz): solid shapes with many flat surfaces

cycle (SYE-kuhl): things happening in the same order again and again. A day's cycle is daytime changing into nighttime and back into daytime.

fossils: bones or other traces of animals and plants that lived long ago

igneous (IHG-nee-uhs) rocks: rocks formed by great heat. Many igneous rocks form deep inside Earth.

lava (LAH-vuh): melted rock on Earth's surface

magma (MAG-muh): melted rock that is inside Earth

metamorphic (MEH-tuh-MOR-fik) rocks: rocks made from other kinds of rock. Heating and squeezing can change an igneous or sedimentary rock into a metamorphic rock.

minerals (MIHN-ur-uhlz): solid substances that form inside Earth and are not alive

plates: large, moving pieces of Earth's crust

rock cycle: the way in which old rocks are changed into new ones

sedimentary (SEH-duh-MEHN-tuh-ree) rocks: rocks made from bits of mud, sand, or small stones

sediments (SEH-duh-muhnts): bits of mud, sand, or small stones

weathering (WEH-thur-ihng): breaking rocks and soil into smaller pieces. Water, wind, and ice are forces that weather rocks.

INDEX

Pages listed in **bold** type refer to photographs.